VIENNA

114 COLOUR PHOTOGRAPHS

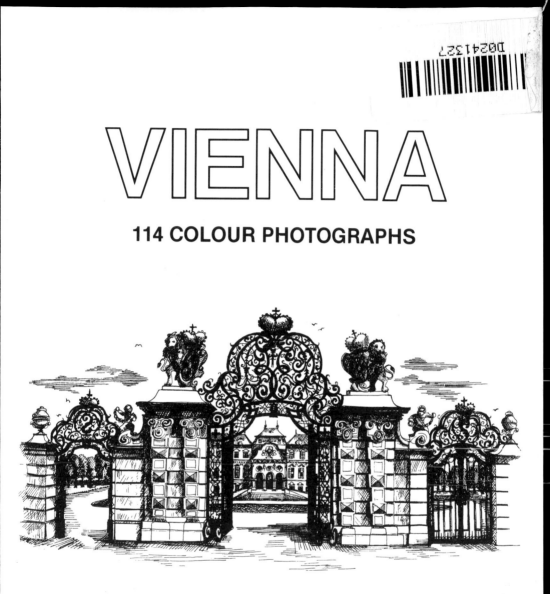

VERLAG

bauer

VIENNA

INTRODUCTION

"I kiss your hand, Madame", "Servus" and a warm "Welcome to Vienna" is what we would like to extend to you at the very beginning of this short introduction to one of the most diversified cities of Europe. Various influences of ethnic, cultural and political kind have resulted in Vienna's unique place in the past as well as the present.

Politically, Vienna is situated right in front of the doors to the East; as may be gathered from the numerous Slavik and Hungarian names in Vienna's telephone directory, the city has always had excellent relations to this part of the world. But Vienna is also at the hub of North and South Europe. Some Viennese words were originally Italian, there are definite traces of the Bohemian and the Polish languages. A short historic survey will give us a more distinct picture of all the complex connections.

A long time ago the **Celts** settled here along the amber route. Later, the **Romans** set up "Vindobona", their garrison against the **Teutons.** The **migration of the peoples** rendered the settlement insignificant for a long time. It was not before 881 that the name "Wenia" was mentioned again in records of Salzburg, a fact documenting the increasing importance of the region as boarderland of the Carolingian, and later the Ottonian empires against the dangerous Avars and Magyars in the East. The **Babenbergs** became margraves and later on dukes of the "Ostarrichi" March. In 1155 they set up their court in Vienna; in 1221 they enacted the oldest municipal consitution transmitted. In 1246 the last Babenberg was killed fighting the Magyars and the dynasty died out. When the Bohemian king Ottokar

Přemysl was defeated by the German king Rudolf von Habsburg, the reign of the **Habsburgs** began. Their fate is closely connected with Vienna's rise to a metropolis. In 1365 Duke Rudolf IV founded the University of Vienna.

After the Turkish advance towards Central Europe had twice — in 1529 and in 1683 — been halted at Vienna, nothing stopped her from becoming a metropolis. Baroque joy of living and the clever reign of **Maria Theresia** (1740—1780) and her son Joseph II (1780—1790) resulted in the most glorious days of the city. Lukas v. Hildebrandt and Johann Bernhard Fischer v. Erlach determined the townscape with magnificent churches and palaces. Haydn, Mozart, Gluck and, later Beethoven and Schubert made Vienna the musical capital of Europe. The occupation by Napoleon led to a short downfall which was followed by another glorious period. In 1814/15 the **Congress of Vienna** assembled the most important sovereigns of Europe. Europe was reorganized, sumptuous festivities were celebrated: "The Congress danced!". The Viennese waltz became a form of art.

During the "Biedermeier" period the contrasts between the wealthy bourgeoisie and the grossly discriminated classes of society aggravated and in 1848 a revolution broke out. Emperor Ferdinand I had to abdicate and the eighteen year old Franz Joseph I succeeded. He was to reign for 68 years. They brought cultural highlights such as the "Golden Age of Operetta" (J. Strauß, F. v. Suppé, C. Zeller, C. M. Ziehrer, K. Millöcker); Brahms, Bruckner and Mahler worked in Vienna; as of 1857 the Ringstrasse was built;

literature and painting florished. At the same time, however, nationalism and separatism began to shake the multinational state and finally lead to a **World War (1914—1918)** that changed Europe completely. Franz Joseph did not live to see the downfall of the Empire (1918), he died in 1916 before the War was over.

The time of crumbling old order and the wistful look back set free incredible cultural powers; the Vienna School of Medicine around Rokitansky and Billroth revolutionized the public health service of the 19th century; Siegmund Freud developed psychoanalysis; poets such as H. Bahr, K. Krauss, A. Schnitzler, H. v. Hofmannsthal and S. Zweig caught up with the heritage of the monarchy; the coffeehouse became a venue for literature, and **Art Nouveau** changed Vienna. Otto Wagner significantly influenced city planning (Stadtbahn). Klimt was the soul of the "Secession" and, together with his pupils Schiele and Kokoschka, paved the way for modern art in Austria. The "Second Viennese School" around Schönberg, Berg and Webern opened up new paths in music.

Today, 40 years after the destructions of World War II, Vienna is changed in many ways. The former metropolis of a large country has became the capital of small and neutral Austria. What is left, however, is the city's important role in the East-West dialogue and her rank in international relations: since 1979 Vienna has been the third seat of the United Nations.

A lot of things Viennese are famous all over the world: Schönbrunn Palace, the Belvedere, the museums, the Vienna Philharmonic Orchestra, the Vienna Boys' Choir, the Opera Ball and the New Year's Concert, the Vienna Festival and the Spanish Riding School, the Sacher torte and the pastries. Still, all the above may hardly explain what is "typical Viennese"; it is merely the facade behind which such contrasts as vivid traditions, "Gemütlichkeit" and modern stress, innovation and traditional roots stand up against any kind of cliché. It is just as difficult to describe the **typical Viennese.** He is generally held to be tolerant and charming. Legend has tried to characterize him in the person of the "Lieber Augustin", a merry fellow who does not loose his good humour despite the plague and wide-spread deaths around him and who — armed with a glass of wine in his hand — fights against destiny and even against death. When Qualtinger and Merz created their "Herr Karl", they had a more critical approach; their theatre figure is an intruding master of the art of living with a pessimistic-whining brutality. However differently the Viennese might have seen themselves, there is one thing most of them have in common: They like to grumble and complain about everything under the sun, they "grouse" and much prefer being "queer birds" and "odd fellows" to being one of the crowd. But please do not confuse "grousing" with indignation! To the contrary! The Viennese only criticize the things they love.

This booklet intends to and, indeed, can do no more than give a survey of the essentials but not of the essence, the nature of Vienna; it should be taken as an invitation to stay in the places you like and to look more closely into the history, the tradition and the present of a charming city.

Detail from the "Wiener Neustädter Altar"   *Josefsaltar*

ST. STEPHEN'S CATHEDRAL

Today's monumental building replaces a Romanesque basilica founded by Duke Heinrich II Jasomirgott in the 12th century. After the fire of 1258 the church was rebuilt in the Romanesque style. The round-arched Giant Gate and the slightly Gothicized Pagan Towers to its sides are still left of this building. The foundation stone for the Gothic church of St. Stephen's was laid by Duke Rudolf IV on April 7, 1359, who was thereafter given the epithet of "the Founder". The southern tower was completed by Hans v. Prachatits in 1433, the nave by Hans Puchsbaum in 1455. The construction of the northern tower was stopped in 1511, most probably due to the Reformation and the close Turkish threat. During the last days of World War II the masterly timbered Gothic roof was destroyed, it has, however, been carefully reconstructed.

The landmark of Vienna, the 137 m tower of St. Stephen's — affectionately called "Steffl" by the Viennese — is held to be one of the most outstanding works of Gothic architecture. At a height of 72 m there is a room which formerly served the fire brigade. Placed in the unfinished northern or "Eagle's Tower" (60 m) since 1957, the **Pummerin** is one of the biggest bells in the world. Made from the metal of captured Turkish canons in 1711 it was originally placed in the southern tower. During the 1945 fire it crashed down and burst. It was re-cast from its pieces; to be heard all over Vienna, the Pummerin now annually rings in the New Year.

The interior of the three-aisle cathedral is spanned by a net vaulting of up to 27 m, supported by 18 columns. The high altar by Johann Jakob Pock (1640—47) is made of black marble. Its centrepiece — painted on pewter slates — depicts the stoning of St. Stephen (first Christian martyr). The **"Wiener Neustädter Altar"** (in the left aisle), a Gothic winged altarpiece dated 1447, is by far more important, however. The middle shrine represents the coronation of the Virgin as well as St. Barbara (with the tower) and St. Catherine (with the wheel). The inner sides of the wings depict the lives of the Virgin and Jesus. The altar carries the letters "AEIOU", the differently interpreted

St. Stephen's Cathedral

The organ pedestal (Master Pilgram)

initials of Frederick III's motto (either: **A**ustria **e**rit **i**n **o**rbe **u**ltima — Austria will not cease to exist until the end of the world; or **A**ustria **e**st **i**mperare **o**rbi **u**niverso — Austria's empire is our universe). Designed by Niclas Gerhaert van Leyden and hewn from red marble, the **sarcophagus of Frederick III** is placed to the front of the right aisle. The tombstone depicts the emperor in full coronation regalia; the side reliefs by Max Valmet and Michael Tischer represent imperial foundations. With its four manuals, 125 stops and with approximately 10,000 pipes the **"big organ"** is one of the greatest in Europe. The oldest part of the organ, the late Gothic **pedestal** (1513), is decorated with a bust of its creator Anton Pilgram. Another self-portrait of Pilgram is the **"Fenstergucker"** underneath the Gothic **pulpit,** which the artist constructed from sandstone in 1514/15. Along its stairs toads and lizzards, symbolizing the evil, are kept back by a dog, representing the good. The parapet features reliefs of the four

The Gothic pulpit

Latin Patriarchs Ambrosius, Hieronymus, Pope Gregor and Augustinus. The popular **"Servant's Madonna"** (1320), close to the main entrance, was also made by this early Gothic artist. The **Capistran pulpit** (around 1430) is another testimony to Gothic architecture; here, the Franciscan monk John Capistran tried to summon forces for a crusade against the Turks in 1451. Worth mentioning are furthermore: the sacred image of the **"Pötsch Madonna"** (1676), a Carpathian-Russian piece of work; the baptisimal font by Ulrich Auer in St. Catherine's Chapel and the Baroque Johann-Nepomuk altar (1723) with a painting by Johann Martin Schmidt ("Kremser Schmidt").

"Fenstergucker"

"Servant's Madonna"

"Big organ"

"Sacred image of the Pötsch Madonna"

Capistran pulpit

Tomb of Frederick III

9

THE DONNER FOUNTAIN
The fountain was constructed by Georg Raphael Donner in 1739; its centrepiece is a statue personifying "Providentia" (Providence).

THE IMPERIAL BURIAL VAULT
Underneath the Capuchin church the members of the Habsburg dynasty are buried in the famous "imperial burial vault" (also **"Capuchin burial vault"**). **Franz Joseph's burial vault** holds the sarcophagus of Emperor Franz Joseph (1830—1916) as well as those of Empress Elisabeth (right) and crownprince Rudolf (left).

THE STATE OPERA

In 1869, the imperial opera house was the first Ringstrassen building to be finished. It was constructed under the influence of the French Renaissance and both, the master planner August von Siccardsburg as well as the interior designer Eduard van der Null, were severely critisized. The mockery of the people drove van der Null to commit suicide, Siccardsburg died from a heart attack shortly afterwards. Non of the two architects lived to see the inauguration of the imperial opera with Mozart's "Don Giovanni" on May 15, 1869. As a result of a bomb attack on March 12, 1945 the building burnt down completely. The

reconstruction according to plans by Erich Boltenstern, Ceno Kosak, Otto Possinger and R. H. Eisenmenger, closely following the historical predecessor, took 10 years. With Beethoven's "Fidelio" conducted by Karl Böhm, the building was inaugurated on November 5, 1955.

The State Opera was headed by great musicians such as Gustav Mahler, Richard Strauss, Franz Schalk and Clemens Krauss; the criticism of the "1.6 million co-directors" — as

Herbert v. Karajan called the Viennese — has made desperate quite a few of them. The Viennese love their opera and perhaps it is this very difficultly for the directors of the house on the Ring that has kept it one of the leading opera houses of the world. A permanent cast with many great singers and the excellent state opera orchestra render possible the high standard of the performances. When the doors of the opera open for the **Opera Ball,** which annually takes place in February, the house becomes the centre of social life.

THE MOZART MEMORIAL
This statue in honour of the great composer Wolfgang Amadeus Mozart was created by Viktor Tilgner in 1896. Born in Salzburg in 1756, Mozart moved to Vienna in 1781 where a lot of his most important works were performed. He was burried at the St. Marx cemetery in Vienna in 1791.

Museum of Fine Arts

P. Bruegel the Elder: "Peasant Wedding", Museum of Fine Arts

THE MUSEUMS OF NATURAL HISTORY AND FINE ARTS

The two museums flanking the Maria Theresia square were built between 1872 and 1881. Gottfried Semper is mainly responsible for the exterior, Karl von Hasenauer for the interior. The ceiling paintings by Hans Canon in the entrance hall of the **Museum of Natural History** most impressively depict the "Cycle of life". The eight sections of the museum convey a unique picture of the history of evolution of animals and plants. Apart from pre-historic and anthropological exhibits and the world-famous collection of meteorites in the mineralogical section there are utensils and art objects of our ancestors (e. g. the renown "Venus of Willendorf", a fertility symbol from the 15th millenium B. C.)

The **Museum of Fine Arts** holds one of the most important art galleries of the world as well as a very extensive collection of sculptures and arts and crafts (extremely famous is Benvenuto Cellini's "Saltcellar" — middle of the 16th century); moreover, there is a coin collection, an Egyptian collection with numerous mummies, a collection of antiques with Greek, Etruscan, Roman and early Christian works of art. A description of only a small part of the overwhelming num-

Rembrandt, "Titus", Museum of Fine Arts

ber of paintings — the round is almost 4 kilometres — would go beyond the scope of this little booklet; we therefore only list some of the masters represented in this museum: Tizian, Tintoretto, Veronese, Caravaggio, Bellotto, Raffael, Velásques, Rubens, Bosch, Rembrandt, Cranach, van Dyck, Holbein, Dürer and Pieter Bruegel. Of the latter, the Flemish master, the Museum of Fine Arts possesses the most extensive complete collection of paintings.

Staircase in the Museum of Fine Arts —

THE PALLAS-ATHENE FOUNTAIN
The most dominant feature of the fountain (design: Th. Hansen) in front of parliament is the statue of Pallas Athene, a work of Karl Kundmann. The goddess of wisdom is flanked by allegorical figures representing legislation and administration (J. Tautenhayn). The gods at her feet symbolize the rivers Danube and Inn, Elbe and Moldau.

THE PARLIAMENT
The magnificent building was designed by Theophil Hansen in the Hellenistic style and built between 1873 and 1883. The main part with its eight Corinthian columns reminds one of a Greek temple. The "Reichsrat" (imperial council) of the Austro-Hungarian monarchy met there. Today, the building is the seat of the National Council as well as the Federal Council.

THE TOWN HALL

Designed by Friedrich Schmidt, the neo-Gothic seat of the mayor was built between 1872 and 1883. The top of the central tower (98 m) is crowned by the 3.4 m figure of the "Rathausmann" (Town Hall man); he is another landmark of Vienna.

The **"Rathaus park",** arranged with love of detail, holds numerous monuments such as those of the great waltz composers Johann Strauß (father) and Joseph Lanner.

THE UNIVERSITY

The edifice was planned by Heinrich Ferstl and built between 1873 and 1883 in the style of the Italian Renaissance. Today it is the main building of the presently oldest German-speaking university, founded by Duke Rudolf IV, the Founder, in 1365.

VOTIVE CHURCH

In 1853 an anarchist's attempt to assassinate Emperor Franz Joseph I failed. As an expression of thanks for his rescue, the neo-Gothic Votiv Church "to our Devine Saviour" was built (1856—1879). It was designed by Heinrich Ferstl. The baptistery holds the tomb of Count Niklas v. Salm (he died around 1533) who defended Vienna against the Turks in 1529. The "Antwerpen altar" (to the right of the high altar) is a Flemish carving (15th century).

THE NATIONAL THEATRE

Built according to Gottfried Semper's and Karl Hasenauer's plans, the theatre was finished in 1888. The "Court and National Theatre", founded by Joseph II in 1776 and called "Hofburg theatre" as of 1821, moved into this new house and has built up the reputation of one of the best German-speaking theatres.

EMPRESS ELISABETH MEMORIAL

Emperor Franz Joseph I's wife Elisabeth was assassinated in Geneva in 1898; the memorial was hewn from marble by Hans Bitterlich (design F. Ollmann) and unveiled in the "Volksgarten in 1907. Elisabeth of Bavaria was born in Munich in 1837 and married to the monarch in 1854.

THE THESEUS TEMPLE

Designed by Peter Nobile and finished in 1823 the Theseus Temple in the "Volksgarten" is an imitation of the Theseion in Athens. It originally held the group "Theseus defeats Minotaur" by Antonio Canova (Museum of Fine Arts). In this century it has hosted a few archaeological (Ephesus findings) and art exhibitions.

The bronze statue "the Winner" was made by Josef Mullner (1921).

THE HELDENPLATZ

The square in front of the Imperial Palace owes its name to two heroes of war history: **Archduke Karl,** who defeated Napoleon I at Aspern in 1809 and **Prince Eugene of Savoy,** the extremely popular military commander. The memorials of the two heroes were made by Anton Fernkorn in the middle of the 19th century.

Austria felt threatened by the Turks who waged a successful war against Venice; therefore, Prince Eugene (1663—1736) set out to support Venice with his troops. He conquered the banate, stormed Belgrade, defeated a Turkish relieving army and finally captured the fortress. (His victory is commemorated in the popular song "Prince Eugene, the noble knight, . . ."). The Treaty of Passarowitz (1718) saw Austria's largest territorial extension ever.

THE IMPERIAL PALACE

The enormous size of this palace is evidence of Austria's power and wealth in times past. A symbol of their 600 year reign, the residence of the Habsburgs reflects the architectural history from the Gothic to the historicizing style of the Ringstrasse. Nevertheless, the various styles of this complex edifice harmonize extremely well.

*Archduke Karl
memorial*

*Prince Eugene
memorial*

The architects Gottfried Semper and Karl v. Hasenauer originally planned a mirror-symetrical second tract. Together with the museums and the Trade Fair Palace on the other side of the Ringstrasse, these edifices were to effect a gigantic "Imperial Forum". This project was only partially realized, however.

Today the Imperial Palace is the seat of the Austrian Federal President (Leopold wing); it houses the Ethnological Museum, parts of the Museum of Fine Arts with a collection of old weapons and musical instruments, the Ephesus Museum, the Treasury, the Austrian National Library, the Spanish Riding School as well as representative meeting rooms for international conferences.

The various museums and the National Library are located in the **"Neue Burg"** (New Palace), ordered by Franz Joseph I and built by Semper and Hasenauer between 1881 and 1913. The **"Michaelertrakt"** had been begun in 1735 according to plans by Joseph Emanuel Fischer v. Erlach; it was only finished in 1893, however. Special attention should be given to the wrestling and falling Hercules sculptures on both sides of the **"Michaelertor"** (gate) and to the fountains at the walls. Their allegorical sculptures represent the "Reign on Land" (Edmund Hellmer) and the "Reign on Sea" (Rudolf Weyr). Emperor Franz Joseph I's study was in the **"Reichs-kanzleitrakt"** (Imperial Chancellery tract), constructed by Lukas von Hildebrandt and Fischer v. Erlach between "Michaelerplatz" and today's "Ballhausplatz" from 1723 to 30. Empress Elisabeth, Franz Joseph's wife, had her appartement in the Baroque **"Amalienburg"**.

"Michaelertrakt"

THE SPANISH RIDING SCHOOL

The "winter riding school" (between "Schweizerhof" and "Stallburg") was finished in 1735 by Joseph Fischer v. Erlach. The pompous Baroque **large hall,** with its gallery held by 16 Corinthian columns, was a brilliant venue for a lot of festive events at the time of the Congress of Vienna. Today it is the background for the performances of the classical art of riding, an art now only cultivated in Vienna. The riders wear historical uniforms. The former "Imperial Riding School" was founded by Charles IV who, in 1580, started to breed a very clever and thoroughbred warm blood in the stud at "Lipizza" (today's Yugoslavia, east of Trieste).

The **Lipizzaner** — they are born black and later turn white with only a few exceptions — are a cross-breed of Andalusians, Arabians and Neapolitans. They not only stood the test in the battlefields but also performed the popular horse ballets and drew the carriage of Emperor Franz Joseph. Today, the unique horses are bred in the federal stud at Piber near Köflach in Styria.

THE AUSTRIAN NATIONAL LIBRARY

The former imperial library at the Josephsplatz was constructed by Johann Bernhard Fischer v. Erlach's son Joseph Emanuel in the years 1723 to 1735 according to the plans of his father. The Grand Hall ranks among the most beautiful rooms of the late Baroque period. Daniel Gran painted the magnificent frescoes: allegoric representations of the various sciences in the dome; a portrait of the owner Emperor Charles IV on the ceiling. The latter's marble statue was placed beneath the dome by Peter and Paul von Strudel, statues of 16 further Habsburgs were arranged around it.

The priceless collections of the National Library comprise more than 2.2 million manuscripts and publications, among them the valuable leather volumes from the inheritance of Prince Eugene, numerous maps, books of music and historical theatre material.

The Austrian Imperial Crown

The Imperial Crown of the Holy Roman Empire

THE SCHWEIZERHOF

In 1275 King Ottokar II Premysl of Bohemia began to build the oldest surviving part of the Imperial Palace. Rudolf II of Habsburg continued the building. During extension work in the Renaissance period, Emperor Ferdinand I ordered the "Schweizertor" (Swiss gate) to be built (1536—1553). The name of the courtyard is derived from the imperial body guard accommodated in this tract; it was Swiss at the time of Maria Theresia. Today the Swiss tract holds the Treasury with its priceless precious objects and miraculous works of goldsmithery and jewellery.

THE TREASURY

The almost unmatched collection goes back to the inheritance of Emperor Maximilian I, and over the years, was enlarged by many a piece of art from the Habsburgs. It comprises a spiritual and a temporal section. Centrepieces are the **insignia of the "Holy Roman Empire of the German Nation"** and the crown of Rudolf II (since 1804 the **Austrian Imperial Crown**). Further exhibits are the jewellery of Empress Maria Theresia, knightly robes of the Order of the "Golden Fleece", the insignia of the Austrian archdukes, the Burgundian treasures from the inheritance of Emperor Maximilian I and many more.

"EMPEROR FRANZ JOSEPH I" AND "EMPRESS ELISABETH"

Today, the two life-size portraits by Winterhalter are placed in the former rooms of the imperial couple.

Franz Joseph I (1830—1916) was both, Emperor of Austria and King of Hungary. After his accession to the throne in 1848 Vienna made a big leap forwards. The old fortifications were demolished; in their place he built the representative Ringstrasse with all its monumental palaces and gardens. The introduction of cultural, social and — last but not least — sanitary institutions bespeaks the humanitarian attitude of the emperor. His wife, Empress Elisabeth from the house of Wittelsbach, — affectio-

nately called "Sissy" by the population — fell victim to an assassination in Geneva in 1898.

MICHAELER CHURCH

Looking towards the church from beneath the dome of the "Michaelertrakt" of the Imperial Palace you will notice the marvellous wrought-iron work in the "Michaelertor". The Michaeler square in front of it is surrounded by significant buildings: the Imperial Palace, the Loos house and the Michaeler church, the former imperial parish church. Some parts originate from the 13th century, it has, however, been repeatedly redesigned and extended. The slim tower is Gothic, the porch was built by Antonio Beduzzi in the Baroque period. In 1792 Ferdinand v. Hohenberg designed the classicistic façade.

The "fall of the angels" is depicted throughout the church; there are a sandstone group by Lorenzo Mattielli at the porch, a collossal painting in the right transept by Michelangelo Unterberger and detailed stucco at the parclose by Karl Georg Merville. The interior of the three-aisle church is full of treasures. In the tower chapel next to the entrance there are parts of frescoes from the 13th century depicting St. Cosima, St. Thomas and St. Damian as well as the "mass of St. Gregor" from the 14th century. The altarpiece of the Johann-Nepomuk altar (1643), depicting the "14 auxiliary saints", was made by T. Pock. The altar of the marvellous vesper chapel has a wooden Pietà (around 1430). The church is also renown for the tombs of important aristocrats.

THE "LOOS HOUSE" ON MICHAELER SQUARE

This residential and business building for the men's wear company Goldmann and Salatsch was built by the Art Nouveau architect Adolf Loos in 1910. The Viennese deemed the design of the façade so revolutionary and dearing that building had to be interrupted for some time. Even Emperor Franz Joseph was annoyed about the frameless windows with "no eyebrows". Loos clearly separated the plainly plastered residential section from the business area lined with Cipollino marble on the outside; with this concept he became a pioneer of the modern functional architecture. The **"Kärntner Bar"** (1st district, Kärntner passage) from the year 1907 is an example of his brilliant interior designs.

Adolf Loos was born in Brünn in 1870. From 1920 to 1922 he was head architect of the housing authority of the municipality of Vienna. Before retreating to Lower Austria, he worked in France and Czechoslovakia. In 1933 he died from a nervous disease in Kalksburg near Vienna and is burried in a tomb of honour at the Vienna Central Cemetary.

THE GRABEN and the COLUMN OF THE HOLY TRINITY (PLAGUE COLUMN)

The name of this former market place was derived from the ditch (= Graben) of the Roman fortification, which was filled up when the city was extended during the 12th century. In fulfilment of an oath made by Emperor Leopold I during the plague, a wooden column was erected in honour of the Holy Trinity in 1679; this column was replaced by an impressive marble one (design M. Rauchmiller) in 1693.

ST. PETER'S CHURCH

Situated next to the Graben, on top of a very old church, we find St. Peter's; consecrated in 1733 it is Vienna's Baroque church richest in treasures. Almost all great masters of the time contributed towards its decoration, among them M. Rottmayr with the dome frescoes and M. Altomonte with his altarpieces. Underneath the altar of the holy family there are the relics of St. Donatus.

Church ''Am Hof''

Civic Armoury   St. Mary's on the Bank

CHURCH "AM HOF"
(Former Jesuit Church)

The Jesuits, called to Vienna in 1551 to pursue the Counter-Reformation, made the old church of the Carmelites "am Hof" Baroque from 1607 to 1610. Today's façade was designed by Carlo Antonio Carlone in 1662. When the order of the Jesuits was abolished, the church of St. Mary became the city parish church.

In 1782 Pope Pius VI travelled to Vienna in order to moderate Joseph II's anti-church reforms; his Easter benediction was pronounced from the balcony of the church. In 1806 Franz II laid down the Imperial Crown of the Roman Empire in this very place.

THE CIVIC ARMOURY

Originally built as an armoury for the people of Vienna it now serves as headquarters of the fire brigade. The three-dimensional decorations of the Baroque façade was made by Lorenzo Matielli.

ST. RUPERT'S CHURCH

The venerable little church is held to be the oldest spiritual building in Vienna. It was founded in 740, the most essential parts date back to the 11th century.

ST. MARY'S ON THE BANK

On the former Danube arm (today's "Salzgries") a Gothic architectural jewel was built on Roman foundations. It is believed that as of the 9th century, houses of prayer for the boatmen stood in this place. The church was first mentioned in a document in 1158. Choir and tower originate from the 14th century. In 1414 the nave and the perforated, filigree spire were completed by Michael Knab.

The Gothic stained-glass windows from the 14th century are very famous; sarcophagus and altar of the Redemptorist Clemens Maria Hofbauer remind us of the patron of the city of Vienna.

FLOATING RESTAURANT
"JOHANN STRAUSS"

THE STATUE OF MARY
Originally, the statue of "Mary the destroyer of sin" stood in the centre of the Marienbrücke (bridge) across the Danube canal. The statue from the year 1909, destroyed during World War II, was replaced by a copy which, due to the traffic, was erected at the side of the lanes.

THE GRIECHENBEISL ''Zum Roten Dachl'' (Griechengasse)
''Lieber Augustin'' is said to have often come to this medieval inn at the time of the plague. The name of the restaurant goes back to the 18th century when many Greek and Levantine businessmen lived in the little streets around it. Famous artists and politicians (Wagner, Strauß, Grillparzer, Nestroy, Lueger, Brahms and Waldmüller) frequented the place, renown for its excellent beer.

THE "ANKER" CLOCK

The bridge-like corridor between the houses Hoher Markt 10 and 11 is fitted with an artistic clock made to the plans of the painter Franz v. Matsch (1913). Every day at noon, 12 figures or pairs of figures — important personalities from the history of Vienna — parade past the old coat of arms of the city (among them Marc Aurel, Charles the Great, Duke Leopold VI, Walter v. d. Vogelweide, Rudolf I, Prince Eugene, Maria Theresia, Joseph Haydn, . . .).

ST. JOSEPH'S COLUMN

In 1702 Leopold I vowed to erect a column in honour of St. Joseph should his son, Josef I take the fortification of Landau and return unharmed. Under Charles IV the original wooden column was replaced by a marble fountain depicting the marriage of Mary and Joseph (figures: A. Corradini), designed by J. E. Fischer v. Erlach.

THE UNIVERSITY CHURCH (Jesuit Church)

In the course of the Counter-Revolution Ferdinand II had the church built for the Jesuits. In 1631 it was consecrated to Mary, to Ignatius of Loyola, the founder of the order, and to the missionary Franz Xaver; between 1703 and 1707 the Jesuit Andrea Pozzo gave the church today's appearance. For the early Baroque façade he created statues of the two holy Jesuits to whom the building was consecrated. In the row above them there are four saints originating from the 17th century (from left to right: St. Catherine, St. Joseph, St. Leopold, St. Barbara). Pozzo also designed the greater part of the interior, the centrepiece of the high altar "the Assumption of the Virgin", the side chapels and the illusionistic ceiling paintings. His marvellously painted make-believe dome may be seen in correct perspective from a white mark close to the last benches. When the order of the Jesuits was dissolved during the enlightened absolutism (1773), the church served for the services of the close-by university. In 1857 the church was returned to the order, which had been re-established by Pope Pius VII in 1814.

THE "KURSALON" in the City Park
Opened in 1867 the "Kursalon" has always been a place for the light music of the waltz and operetta era. Here Eduard Strauß and the excellent military bands of the monarchy used to give their famous "promenade concerts".

THE JOHANN-STRAUSS MEMORIAL in the City Park
A private committee together with the municipality of Vienna raised the funds for E. Hellmer's bronze statue of the composer as well as for the marble relief.
Johann Strauß (son) was born in Vienna in 1825 and — after a turbulent and glorious life in the service of waltz and operetta — died in his hometown in 1899.

THE GRAND HALL OF THE VIENNA MUSIKVEREIN

The Grand or "Golden" Hall of the house of the "Gesellschaft der Musikfreunde" — abbreviated to "Musikverein" — was built by Theophil Hansen between 1867 and 1869; it is without doubt the centre of musical life in Vienna. It is quasi the home of the Vienna Philharmonic Orchestra whose **New Year's concert** is broadcast on TV to many countries. Musicians from all over the world have guest performances under the gilt caryatids and — just as the audience — praise the incomparable acoustics. Founded in 1817 the "Gesellschaft der Musikfreunde" has an extensive collection on the history of music, inestimable autographs, books of music, musical instruments and memorials.

CHURCH OF ST. CHARLES

In 1713 the plague raged through Vienna once more and Charles VI vowed to build a church in the honour of St. Charles Borromäus once it was over. This church is probably Vienna's most important spiritual building of Baroque style. Begun by Johann Bernhard Fischer v. Erlach in 1716 it was completed by his son Joseph Emanuel in 1739. Johann Christoph Mader made the two 33 m **triumphal columns** modelled on the Trajan column in Rome; the spiral reliefs relate the life of St. Charles. The columns, the elements of the façade and the 72 m dome harmonize in a most sophisticated way. The interior was decorated by the greatest masters of the time: Michael Rottmayr (frescoes), Daniel Gran (altarpiece in the baptistery), J. B. Fischer v. Erlach (high altar).

PALAIS SCHWARZENBERG

In 1716 Prince Adam v. Schwarzenberg acquired J. Lukas v. Hildebrandt's unfinished building. Until 1728 it was completed by Johann Bernhard and, later on, his son Joseph Emanuel Fischer v. Erlach. The valuable frescoes by Daniel Gran were mostly destroyed during World War II.

THE FOUNTAIN (HOCHSTRAHL-BRUNNEN) in Schwarzenberg square

The fountain was paid for by Anton Gabrielli who used some of his money earned building the first Viennese aqueduct (1873). In 1906 it was transformed into a luminous fountain. The number and the grouping of the individual rays correspond to the number of weeks, months and days; 12 high rays symbolize the months, 24 low rays the hours. When Vienna was **liberated** by the Red Army the **memorial** behind the fountain was erected (1945). It was planned and executed by Russian officers. The statue of a Red Guardsman (12 m) stands on a 20 m column in front of a balustrade.

42

Lower Belvedere

BELVEDERE PALACE

Prince Eugene of Savoy, victor over the Turks and "secret" emperor, ordered Johann Lukas von Hildebrandt to build this Baroque summer residence. It consists of two palaces and a splendid park laid out by the Bavarian Dominique Girard. In 1725 the complex was mostly finished. The Upper

Upper Belvedere

Belvedere served representative purposes, the Lower was the Prince's summer residence. When he died his heiress sold it to the Habsburgs. In 1777 Joseph II transferred his imperial collection of paintings to this building. In 1806 the collection of Ambras Palace (from the Tyrol, which had become Bavarian under Napoleon) was added. In 1890 both collections were transferred to the newly erected Museum of Fine Arts on the Ring. As of 1894 the Upper Belvedere was the temporary residence of the heir apparent, Francis Ferdinand, later on murdered in Sarajevo. The composer Anton Bruckner lived in the custodian wing until he died (1896). On May 15, 1955 the Austrian State Treaty was signed in the Great Marble Hall of the Upper Belvedere; this Treaty ended the occupation of Austria by the victorious powers of the World War. Austria was free again.

Today the Austrian Gallery can dispose of the entire Belvedere. The Lower Belvedere houses the **Austrian Baroque Museum** with sculptures and paintings from the 17th/18th centuries, in the orangery of the Lower Belvedere there is the **Museum of Medieval Austrian Art** with works from the 12th to

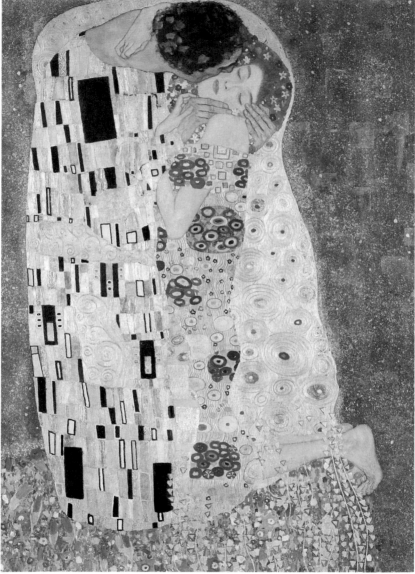

Gustav Klimt: The Kiss

the 16th centuries. The **Gallery of the 19th and the 20th Century** in the Upper Belvedere comprises sections for classicism, Biedermeier, the Ringstrassen era, Art Nouveau and the most extensive collection of works by Klimt, Schiele and Kokoschka.

THE SECESSION

In founding the "Viennese Secession" in 1897, engaged Viennese artists broke away from the "isms" of academic tradition. In 1897/98 Otto Wagner's pupil Josef M. Olbrich built the exhibition pavillon (the "Secession") of this movement, whose members were Josef Hoffmann, **Gustav Klimt** and other important **Art Nouveau** artists. A laurelbush-shaped bronze dome rests on the square elements of the "temple of art".

ART NOUVEAU HOUSES

In order to clearly st his demand for p chrome façades, C Wagner, the great Vi nese city architect at turn of the century, e ted two residential b dings, partly at his o cost. House no. 38 v decorated by Kolo Mo: the façade of the **"ma lica house",** no. 40, presses with strik floral ornaments.

Naiad fountain in the park of Schönbrunn Palace

SCHÖNBRUNN PALACE

Hunting on the site of today's palace around 1619, Emperor Matthias discovered the "beautiful spring" (schöner Brunnen) after which the residence was to be named. In 1695 Leopold I ordered Johann Bernhard Fischer v. Erlach to construct a palace on the site of the "Kotterburg", which had been destroyed by the Turks; it was supposed to even excel Versailles. Due to financial reasons a smaller plan was carried out, however. Under Maria Theresia the building was extended by Nicolaus Pacassi from 1744 to 49. Laid out in the classical French manner, the gardens got their present appearance in 1765. With their walks of trees, their avenues, flower carpets, lawns and fountains they rank among the most beautiful gardens of Europe. In 1752 the **Schönbrunn Palace Zoo** was built, later on the Roman ruins (1778), the pavillon **"to the beautiful spring"** (1779), the **Neptune fountain** (1780) at the foot of the hill on which F. v. Hohenberg erected the **Gloriette** in 1775, and the **palm house** in 1883. Built in 1749 the palace theatre received its beautiful rococo decoration in 1767. Haydn and Mozart had performances there. Located in the former winter riding school, the **Imperial Coach Collection** is one of the largest collections of historical state and everyday carriages. The most beautiful piece of the collection is doubtlessly the Imperial Carriage, the state carriage of the court of Vienna. Ever since Maria Theresia Schönbrunn was the favourite residence. Historical events took place in many of the 1441 rooms and halls. Here, Joseph II married Isabella of Parma in 1760 and his second wife Josefa of Bavaria in 1765. In 1805/06 and again in 1809 the Palace was Napoleon's headquarter, and in 1814/15 the Congress of Vienna danced there. Schönbrunn was Emperor Franz Joseph I's (1830—1916) place of birth and of death. Charles I, Austria's last emperor, abdicated there in 1918 and thus ended the monarchy in Austria.

47

Schönbrunn Palace

48

Palm house

Gloriette and Neptune fountain

Gloriette

The drawing room of the empress

The yellow room

The ceremonial room was used for special occasions. Remarkable is the life-size portrait of Maria Theresia from the school of van Meytens

The Grand Gallery

Designed for representative purposes the room is still used for State Receptions. Guglielmi's frescoes are a homage to Maria Theresia.

Emperor Franz Joseph I's bedroom

The markedly bourgeois furniture was in line with the spartanic-military lifestyle of the monarch, who died here in 1916.

The Marie-Antoinette Room

The million room

The marvellous roco[co]
decoration is said to h[ave]
cost one million guld[en].
The room is fitted w[ith]
valuable sorts of f[ine]
wood, 260 Indian min[ia-]
tures and select furnit[ure]

The large Rosa room

The room is named a[fter]
the painting by Jo[seph]
Rosa. Remarkable [are]
some Chinese pieces [as]
well as the rococo cl[ock]
on a pedestal.

The Napoleon room

The room served as [a]
bedroom to Maria The[re-]
sia and later on to Na[po-]
leon I. Napoleon's s[on]
the Duke of Reichst[adt]
died here in 1832.

"Beautiful spring" (Schöner Brunnen)

Lion in the zoological garden

Imperial Coach Collection, "Imperial Carriage"

THE STRUDELHOF STAIRS
The beautiful flight of outdoor stairs between Liechtensteinstrasse and Strudel-hofgasse gained world-fame because of Heimito v. Doderer's novel (1951).

SPITTELBERG
The typical Viennese suburban lanes and houses on the Spittelberg (in today's 7th district) date back to the time around 1800.

THE ''HUNDERTWASSER'' HOUSE. With this residential building Friedensreich Hundert-wasser materialized a vision of new, ecological housing. In 1985 tens of thousands of Viennese visited the building shortly before it was finished.

THE PRATER

In 1766 Joseph II opened the formerly imperial hunting grounds in the Prater to the public. The area developed into a well-liked recreation area of the Viennese. Coffeehouses, stores and restaurants opened and very soon the **"Wurstelprater"** (public amusement park) came into being, offering a lot of amusement for young and old people. In 1840 Basilio Calafati installed his famous merry-go-round "tö the Great Chinese" and the "Wurstel", the famous hand puppet, lived through many incredible adventures. In 1897 the Giant Ferris Wheel was erected. The "Wurstelprater" was badly damaged during the last days of the War (1945) and rebuilt in a modernized fashion: the miniature railway (**"Liliputbahn"**) again connects the Giant Ferris Wheel and the Prater stadium; there are big dippers, swings, merry-go-rounds, shooting galleries, ghost trains and distorting mirrors and he who wants to left off steam can hit the "Watschenmann".

GIANT FERRIS WHEEL

This landmark was built by the English engineer Walter B. Basset in 1896/97. During the last days of the War in 1945 all carriages and the engine were destroyed, but only one year later the Giant Ferris Wheel again turned around its axis with a diameter of half a metre and a length of more than ten metres. The diameter of the Wheel itself is 61 m, its very top is 64.75 m. The total construction with its 120 spokes weighs 430.05 tons. Enjoy the marvellous view from the slowly moving carriages.

At the **Praterstern,** an important traffic junction, there is the Admiral **Tegetthoff memorial** (K. Kundmann); Tegetthoff defeated the Italians in the naval battle of Lissa (1866).

ISLAMIC CENTRE
Centre of the Islamic culture in Vienna is the mosque, built between 1975 and 79.

VIENNA INTERNATIONAL CENTRE
In 1979 the United Nations made Vienna their third seat besides New York and Geneva. Between 1973 and 1979 the **Vienna International Centre** was built to the plans of Johann Stabler. It is a large construction of glass and reinforced concret. Presently, approx. 3800 UN employees from more than 100 countries work there. When it became independent, Austria joined the Organization in 1955. Vienna has been the headquarters of the IAEO, the International Atomic Energy Agency, since 1957 and of the UNIDO, the United Nations Industrial Development Organization, since 1967.

THE DANUBE PARK
The park is approx. one square kilometre and was laid out on the occasion of the Vienna International Garden Exhibition in 1964. Situated between the Old and the New Danube, it has become a well-liked recreational area of the Viennese. The central sight of the park is the Danube Tower.

THE DANUBE TOWER
The 252 m tower was built under the supervision of Hannes Lintl and Robert Krapfenbauer. Within a few seconds the elevator takes you up to the terrace in 165 m. Above this terrace there are a café and a restaurant. They slowly turn around the axis and offer a beautiful view over Vienna.

Hauermandl

GRINZING

Grinzing was incorporated into Vienna in 1892. Of all the Viennese Heurigen districts such as Sievering, Nußdorf, Salmannsdorf and Neustift am Walde, Grinzing has best preserved the character of a winegrower's village. The larger part of the picturesque village centre dates back to the 16th and 17th centuries.

The grapes from the surrounding vineyards are made into "Heuriger", a wine said to have turned many a good fellow into a philosopher.

Heurigen courtyard

Grinzing village church

The BEETHOVEN HOUSE in the Probusgasse is situated close to the one on the Marktplatz 2. Due to the medicinal springs in the vicinity, Beethoven lived here during the year 1802; here, 25 years before his death, Beethoven composed the "Heiligenstadt Testament", this pathetic manifesto of his experience of life.

The Beethoven house on the Marktplatz 2

View of Vienna

KAHLENBERG and LEOPOLDSBERG are the last elevations of the Vienna Woods and thus of the Alps. From here the Christian troops set out for their decisive battle against the Turks in 1683. In the morning a mass was celebrated in which Jan Sobieski, the king of Poland, officiated as ministrant. The relieving armies fought a victory of historical imminence; the pending islamization of Europe was avoided.

THE KAHLENBERG

In 1629 the order of the Camaldolese founded a hermitage on the otherwise unsettled hill; it was destroyed by the Turks in 1683. On this site we now find the Baroque **St. Joseph's church** in which a copy of the **"Black Madonna"** of Tschenstochau and the Sobieski chapel remind us of Poland's important role in the victory over the Turks in 1683.

<--

THE LEOPOLDS-BERG

In 1679 Emperor Leopold I laid the foundation-stone of a chapel consecrated to the holy Babenberg Margrave Leopold III, it was later destroyed by the Turks. After the victory over the invaders the emperor vowed to restore the little church; the hill on which it stands was named after the Saint. The so-called "Babenberg fortress" had burnt down during the first Turkish invasion in 1529 and had not been rebuilt.

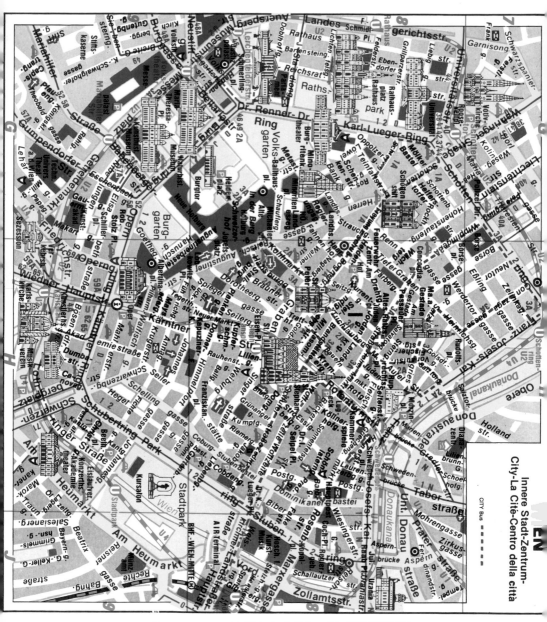

Innere Stadt-Zentrum-
City-La Cité-Centro della città

CITY Bus -------